First published 2016.

Pitkin Publishing
The History Press
The Mill, Brimscombe Port
Stroud, Gloucestershire GL5 2QG
www.thehistorypress.co.uk

Enquiries and sales: 01453 883300
Email: sales@thehistorypress.co.uk

Text written by Cate Ludlow.
The author has asserted their moral rights.

Designed by Chris West.

British Library Cataloguing in Publication Data.
A Catalogue record for this book is available from
the British Library.

Publication in this form © Pitkin Publishing 2016.

ISBN 978-1-84165-734-9

With most grateful thanks to David Freeman and Paul Courtenay

'The first time you meet Winston
you see all his faults, and the
rest of your life you spend
in discovering his virtues.'

Edith, Dowager Countess of Lytton

'I prefer to remember the Guv'nor
as history will without doubt do –
as Mr Churchill, an Englishman.'

Norman McGowan, Churchill's valet

'We are all worms. But I do
believe that I am a glowworm.'

Winston Churchill

Contents

CHAPTER
ONE

Family and Childhood

1 Winston (after the father of the 1st Duke of Marlborough) Leonard (after his grandfather) Spencer-Churchill was born on 30 November 1874 in a bedroom-turned-temporary-cloakroom at Blenheim Palace, during a ball. His mother went into labour whilst dancing.

2 His father described him as 'wonderfully pretty and very healthy'.

3 He was born just seven months after his parents' wedding ...

4 Winston's family was aristocratic: his paternal grandfather, uncle and cousin were all dukes. If his cousin hadn't had children, Churchill would have become the 10th Duke of Marlborough.

5 The Dukedom of Marlborough is one of the few English titles that has been allowed (on one occasion, at least) to pass down the female line in the absence of a son – which is how the Spencer in Spencer-Churchill came to be added.

6

His family's seat, Blenheim
Palace, had 200 rooms and
eighty-eight members of
staff (including twelve cooks),
but only a single bathroom.

7

Churchill's mother used
to join the Blenheim tours.
To her great amusement,
she once overheard a visitor
saying, 'My, what poppy eyes
these Churchills have got!'

8 Churchill's father, Lord Randolph Spencer-Churchill, was a parliamentary star. As Herbert Asquith later put it: 'Randolph was irresistible. He had incomparably more charm, more wit. But Winston is by far the better man.'

9 Alternatively, Randolph was described by Lord Derby as 'scarcely a gentleman, and probably more or less mad'.

10 Churchill once estimated he'd had less than five real conversations with his father. He was overheard telling his own son, home from school, 'I have talked to you more this holiday than my father talked to me in his whole life.'

11 Churchill's mother, Jeanette 'Jennie' Jerome, was born in Brooklyn, New York. She was American, and it's possible that she had some Native American ancestry.

12 The most famous description of Winston's beautiful mother was that she had 'more of the panther than the woman in her look'.

13 Jennie agreed to marry Churchill's father just three days after being introduced to him at a party held on a warship.

14 'My mother shone for me like the Evening Star,' wrote Winston. 'I loved her dearly – but at a distance.'

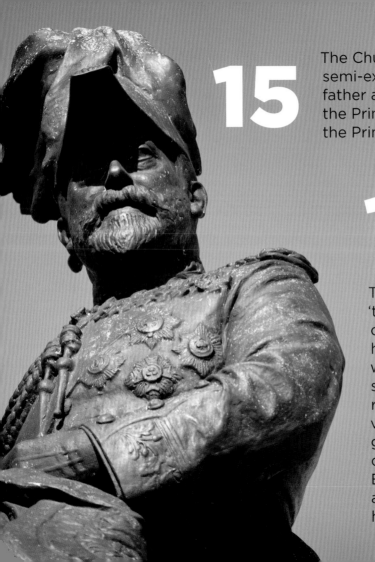

15

The Churchills were forced into semi-exile in Ireland after Winston's father attempted to blackmail the Prince of Wales: in response, the Prince challenged him to a duel.

16

The Churchills lived at 'the Little Lodge' on the edge of Phoenix Park, Dublin. Two high-ranking civil servants were stabbed to death there shortly after they left. Churchill remembered one of the victims, Under Secretary Burke, giving him a toy drum as a child. His mother later visited Burke's murderers in prison, an experience which spurred her interest in prison reform.

17 One of Winston's first memories was the Dublin theatre burning down, leaving nothing but a set of keys from the incinerated manager's pocket. He later wrote that 'he wanted very much to see the keys, but the request does not seem to have been well received.'

18 Churchill's only sibling John (known as Jack) was born in Ireland.

19 Churchill loved his nurse Mrs Elizabeth Ann Everest, whom he called 'Woom' or 'Woomany'. In *My Early Life*, he wrote, 'She had been my dearest and most intimate friend during the whole of the twenty years I had lived.'

20 Churchill was with his nurse when she died; he paid for her funeral, wreath and gravestone.

21 As a child, Winston owned over 1,500 toy soldiers; according to Churchill scholar Michael Paterson, they were most probably made in Germany!

22

Rosa Lewis, the 'Duchess of Jermyn Street' and King Edward VII's favourite cook, once worked for the Churchills; she allegedly shouted, 'Hop it, copper knob!' at Winston when he raided her kitchen.

23

Churchill and his brother Jack once built a large fort, with a moat and a working drawbridge; they also built a working catapult, which they used to fire apples at a cow.

24

Winston nearly died of double pneumonia as a child.

25

Pneumonia struck again as an adult: Churchill was one of the first people in history to be treated with M&B (May & Baker) 693, sulfonamide antibiotics. He took them with whisky, declaring 'man does not live by M&B alone!'

M & B 693

26

Winston's first book was called *Reading Without Tears*. He hid in the woods from the governess who was to teach it to him.

27 Churchill went to three schools: St George's, Ascot, opposite the racecourse (which he hated); Brunswick (now closed) in Hove, run by two sisters called Kate and Charlotte Thomson; and Harrow, whose uniform is still a straw or top hat, a tailcoat for best and a cane. As Churchill put it, 'I am all for Public Schools, but I do not want to go there again.'

28 Churchill's St George's school reports read 'does not understand the meaning of hard work', 'rather greedy at meals', and 'very bad – is a constant trouble to everybody and is always in some scrape or other'.

29 Fellow St George's pupil Maurice Baring remembered Winston stealing the headmaster's straw hat and kicking it 'to pieces'.

30 He was removed from St George's when his nurse noticed caning cuts on his buttocks and reported them to his mother.

31 Winston once performed in drag in the Brunswick play. His character was called 'Lady Bertha', and his mother said he looked 'so pretty'.

32 According to Martin Gilbert's fabulous *Churchill: A Life*, Churchill was once stabbed by a fellow Brunswick pupil after they fell out during an art exam. 'What adventures Winston does have!' his father wrote.

33 Churchill was rated the worst pupil in his class at Brunswick for 'Conduct'. When he entered Harrow he was the lowest-scoring boy in the lowest form in his entire year.

34 'Spencer-Churchill' appears in Harrow's punishment book in 1892. He got seven strokes of the cane for 'breaking into premises and causing damage'. (He and some friends had smashed all the remaining windows in a derelict factory building.)

35 Once, when Winston was being caned by an older boy at school, he cried out, 'I shall be a greater man than you!' He got two further strokes of the cane for his trouble.

36 Winston's naughtiness at school echoed his father, who once took a bulldog into his class at Eton. Winston bought a 'very tame & affectionate' bulldog when he was at school too.

37 Churchill's childhood dancing teacher, Vera Moore, appears in the first volume of *Finest Hour* (The Churchill Centre's award-winning quarterly journal): 'I used to think he was the naughtiest small boy in the world,' she said.

38 At school he would correct his teachers if they misquoted Shakespeare.

39 Churchill once startled Laurence Olivier with his perfect recall of complete speeches from *Henry IV* and *Henry V*.

40 Richard Burton once described hearing a 'dull rumble' from the stalls during a performance of *Hamlet*. It was Churchill, 'speaking the lines with me'. 'He knew the play absolutely backwards,' Burton said.

41 Churchill won a prize at Harrow for reciting 1,200 lines of poetry without a single mistake.

42 Churchill's first memory was of one of his grandfather's speeches. He could still quote the line 'and with a withering volley he shattered the enemy's line' decades later.

43 Churchill was the Public Schools' Fencing Champion in 1892, noted for his 'quick and dashing attack'.

44 Winston won his school rifle-shooting competition (and was still a crack shot as an adult, according to his bodyguard Walter Thompson). Weapons available to the Harrow Rifle Corps, of which Churchill was a member, included a Maxim machine gun.

45 Churchill hated Latin: his Latin entrance exam for Harrow was famously a blank page with his name, an ink blot and the Roman numeral I (in brackets) drawn on it.

46 At prep school his first Latin lesson had also ended badly when he was instructed on the correct way to talk to a table. 'But I never do!' he had replied, much to the master's annoyance.

47 Eventually a friend translated Churchill's Latin homework for him in return for English essays dictated by Winston.

48 At Sandhurst Winston's Latin score was just 362 of a possible 2,000 marks.

49 As a teenager he spent three months in bed after leaping from a bridge in order to catch on to a tree; he woke up in bed three days later, after dropping 29ft into the chasm.

50 Seventy years later, as Martin Gilbert reveals, an X-ray showed that Churchill fractured his thigh in the fall.

51 Churchill took heroin as a teenager: it was prescribed for toothache at the time.

52 In January 2015, the *Daily Mail* reported the discovery, in a Gloucestershire barn, of an 1892 photograph showing a seventeen-year-old Churchill and his contemporaries at Harrow. Only two boys in the image outlived him: more than half died in the world wars.

53 Two of his classmates fought in Churchill's disastrous campaign at Gallipoli; one became Emperor Hirohito's interpreter, and another was tried at the Old Bailey for fraud.

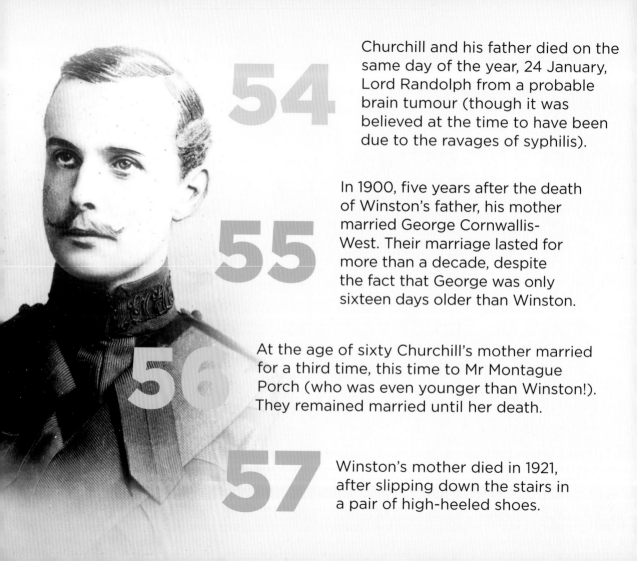

54 Churchill and his father died on the same day of the year, 24 January, Lord Randolph from a probable brain tumour (though it was believed at the time to have been due to the ravages of syphilis).

55 In 1900, five years after the death of Winston's father, his mother married George Cornwallis-West. Their marriage lasted for more than a decade, despite the fact that George was only sixteen days older than Winston.

56 At the age of sixty Churchill's mother married for a third time, this time to Mr Montague Porch (who was even younger than Winston!). They remained married until her death.

57 Winston's mother died in 1921, after slipping down the stairs in a pair of high-heeled shoes.

CHAPTER
TWO

Military Career and Adventures

58 It took Churchill three attempts to get into Sandhurst, but he graduated near the top of his class and became the Colonel of the Regiment in 1941.

59 Winston came first in the history section of his entrance exam to Sandhurst.

60 Winston famously lost an expensive watch, a present from his father, in the Sandhurst river. He hired twenty-three soldiers and a fire engine to dam and drain the river so he could reclaim it.

61 Winston learnt to jump on or off a moving horse (without a saddle) in the cavalry, and to gallop over an obstacle with his hands behind his back.

62 He scored 290 out of a possible 300 points on his final riding exam at Sandhurst.

63 Winston's regiment, the 4th Hussars, took part in the Charge of the Light Brigade.

64

It took Churchill six years to pay for his cavalry uniform.

65

Whilst in the cavalry Winston was implicated in a horse-racing swindle and accused of acts of 'gross immorality of the Oscar Wilde type'. The allegations were dismissed in the resulting libel suit, and Churchill was awarded damages of £400.

66 Speaking of Oscar Wilde types, Boris Johnson's biography shares one of the best Churchill stories. Churchill was told that one of his ministers had been caught in a compromising position with a young guardsman on a Hyde Park bench at 3 a.m. 'In this weather?' replied Churchill. 'Good God, man! Makes you proud to be British!'

67 In 1917 Churchill sued Oscar Wilde's lover Bosie, Lord Alfred Douglas, for libel: Douglas falsely claimed that Churchill had used his position as Minister to manipulate stock prices, and was sent to prison for six months.

68 Churchill was shot at in Cuba just after his twenty-first birthday.

69 In 1897 Winston helped to put down a Pathan revolt on the borders of Afghanistan. 'I have seen several things which have not been very pretty,' he wrote to his mother. 'I saw a great many people killed and wounded and heard a great many bullets strike all round or whistle by.'

70 Churchill was Mentioned in Dispatches for his 'courage and resolution' during the Pathan revolt.

71 Churchill's commander in the Pathan revolt had one of the best names in British military history: Sir Bindon Blood. His ancestor, Colonel Blood, once tried to steal the Crown Jewels.

72

To his horror, the first edition of Churchill's book about the Pathan revolt, *The Malakand Field Force*, went straight to press without an adequate proofread, and thus was (and is) riddled with errors.

73

Intriguingly, Churchill used the pen name 'Winston S. Churchill' to avoid confusion with a popular American novelist called Winston Churchill! The two even went for dinner; the bill was sent to the wrong Mr Churchill.

74 Churchill's advice to his namesake, the American author Winston Churchill, was this: 'I mean to be Prime Minister of England. It would be a great lark if you were President at the same time!'

75 Churchill took part in one of the last cavalry charges by the British Army, during the final stages of the Battle of Omdurman, in the Sudan, in 1898.

76 Winston's small force of cavalry thought they were charging 100 men; in fact, there were at least 1,500 waiting in the stream bed. Churchill was so close to the enemy that he actually touched one man with his pistol as it fired. He later wrote, 'I suppose it was the most dangerous 2 minutes I shall live to see.'

77 Nearly a quarter of Churchill's regiment was killed or wounded in the charge at Omdurman. One man later recovered his brother's watch: pierced by an enemy lance, it was frozen at the exact time of the charge.

78 After the Battle of Omdurman, Churchill gave a strip of skin from his right arm – taken off, without anaesthetic, using a razor – to a friend who needed a skin graft.

79 Churchill was the longest-lived member of the charge at Omdurman; Sir Hugh Bateman Protheroe-Smith, who was second longest, died at the age of eighty-nine.

80 Coincidentally, a Harrow contemporary of Churchill's, Herbert Basil Rivington, became a missionary to Omdurman.

81 The commander of the Omdurman forces was Sir Herbert Kitchener. Churchill and Kitchener did not get on, particularly after Churchill informed readers of *The River War* that Kitchener had rifled a tomb and taken his enemy's head as a trophy. (He stored it in a petrol can, and was reportedly planning to use the skull as a cup.)

82

Churchill later described Kitchener's feelings for him as 'a case of dislike before first sight'.

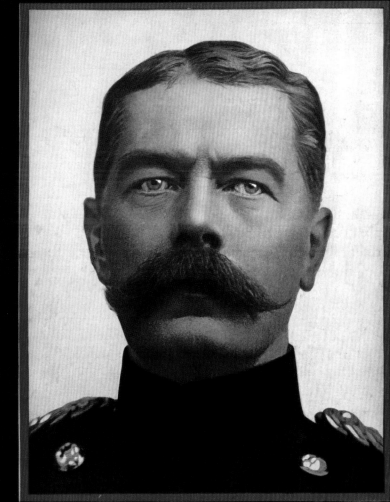

83

Churchill dislocated his shoulder disembarking in India, meaning he could never again swing a cavalry sword (or a tennis racket) and had to play polo (which he played every day) with one arm strapped to his side.

84 In 1899 Churchill scored three goals to win the famous and extremely competitive Inter-Regimental Tournament polo championship, despite having re-dislocated his arm falling down some steps the night before.

85 On one occasion, he wrote, his damaged shoulder nearly popped back out of joint after he made 'a too expansive gesture' in the House of Commons.

86 Winston's pony in India was called Firefly. Firefly's favourite food, according to a letter home from Churchill, was either biscuits or bread and butter.

87 Winston gave up playing polo on his fiftieth birthday.

88 He is the only Prime Minister to have been shot at on four continents: Asia, Africa, Europe and off Central America. He is also the only Prime Minister to wear military uniform whilst in office.

89 In South Africa, on 15 November 1899, Boers wrecked Winston's train by placing a huge stone on the tracks. Both driver and officers thought he'd win a VC for his bravery in the fight that ensued.

90 Churchill wrote for various newspapers throughout his early adventures. He reportedly shouted, as the Boers attacked, 'Keep cool, men! This will be interesting for my paper!'

91 He was taken prisoner by the Boers, and spent his twenty-fifth birthday in the States Model School prison (now a library). Shortly afterwards he climbed over a wall by the loos to escape; he then hid aboard a train, down a coal mine and in a wool truck, eventually ending up back at his own lines on Christmas Eve.

92 Some of his fellow prisoners later escaped by tunnelling under the classrooms of the States Model School. Their pyjamas, playing cards and digging tools were found in the tunnel after their escape.

93

Mr Dewsnap, one of the men who hid Churchill down the mine, was from Oldham, where Churchill had just (unsuccessfully) stood for election! 'They'll all vote for you next time,' he whispered to Winston.

94 South African mine owner Mr Dewsnap's wife was in the gallery when Churchill returned to Oldham to give a second election speech. He won by 230 votes.

95 On his first night hiding in the coal mine in South Africa Winston's only source of light (a candle) was eaten by rats whilst he was sleeping.

96

Churchill gave away his coal-mine hiding place by smoking a cigar: the smell floated to the outside. Luckily, the boy who followed the scent thought Churchill was a ghost and ran away.

97 Churchill's provisions aboard the wool truck he hid on in South Africa included a cup (well – three bottles) of tea.

98 The Boer reward for capturing Churchill was £25, 'dead or alive'. His official description ended: 'small and hardly noticeable moustache, talks through his nose, and cannot pronounce the letter s properly.'

99 Winston practised tongue-twisters throughout his life to improve his lisp, and later wore dentures designed to help with his speech.

100 Churchill told his speech doctor, Sir Felix Semon, about his plans to be a statesman. 'Augusta,' Semon told his wife, 'I have just seen the most extraordinary young man I have ever met.'

101

Churchill's commander after his Boer War escape was Sir Charles Warren, the man who (as chief of the Met) sent bloodhounds over London looking for Jack the Ripper.

102

Some true-crime researchers have identified Churchill's friend Walter Sickert as Jack the Ripper. The pair often painted together.

103

Churchill's mother brought
a hospital ship to the Boer
conflict in South Africa.
One of her first patients was
her own son Jack: on his
very first skirmish a bullet
had whistled past Winston's
head and hit Jack in the calf.

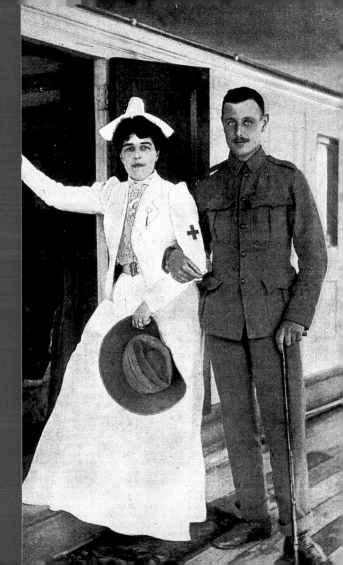

104

One of the guns aboard HMS *Terrible* was named after Churchill's mother.

105

Churchill and his mother both visited Ladysmith after it was relieved.

106

Winston Churchill helped to liberate British prisoners at the end of the Boer War, raising his hat and cheering as the prisoners 'tore like madmen' to welcome him.

107

Churchill once rode through the Boer lines on a bicycle.

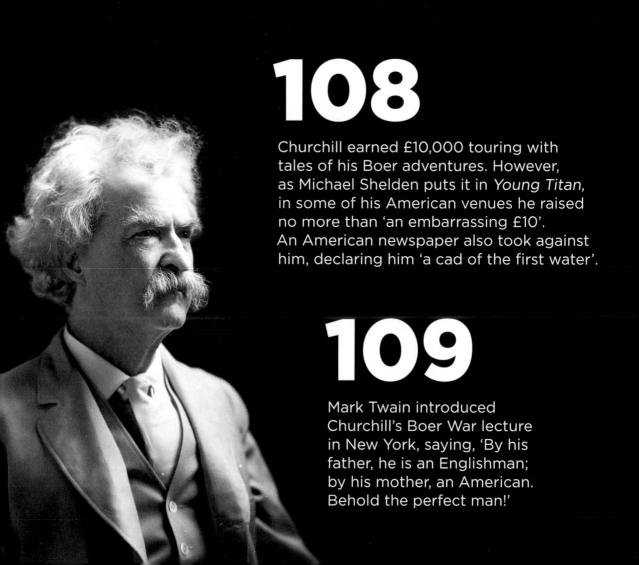

108

Churchill earned £10,000 touring with tales of his Boer adventures. However, as Michael Shelden puts it in *Young Titan*, in some of his American venues he raised no more than 'an embarrassing £10'. An American newspaper also took against him, declaring him 'a cad of the first water'.

109

Mark Twain introduced Churchill's Boer War lecture in New York, saying, 'By his father, he is an Englishman; by his mother, an American. Behold the perfect man!'

110 American audiences liked to cheer the Boers and boo the Brits during Churchill's Boer War lecture series.

111 Churchill's US tour was managed by Major Pond (James Pond, no less). Other clients included Arthur Conan Doyle, Frederick Douglass and Ann Eliza Young, who gave a blockbuster tour about her scandalous life as the nineteenth wife of Mormon President Brigham Young.

112 Major Pond, Churchill's manager, began his career helping slaves escape on the Underground Railroad. He won the Medal of Honour for firing a Howitzer at a group of attacking raiders. However, Pond and Churchill did not get on, Churchill calling Pond a 'vulgar Yankee impresario'.

113 In 1907 Churchill took a train across Africa. His haul of big game included a rhinoceros, three rare white rhinos, a hippo and a crocodile (the shooting of which caused 'hundreds and hundreds of crocodiles, of all sorts and sizes' to rush 'madly into the Nile').

114 He travelled all the way to the source of the Nile and beyond, some of the way by bicycle, meeting countless tribes as he went. In Mruli, for example, 'four hundred wild spearmen, casting aside their leopard skins, danced naked [before him] in the dusk.'

115 Churchill collected butterflies throughout his life, and even raised one rare species in his own butterfly house. His Indian collection was tragically eaten by a rat, but in the jungles of Uganda he found (and held) 'butterflies as big as birds'.

116

Churchill visited the pyramids of Egypt with Gertrude Bell and Lawrence of Arabia. When Lawrence later came to tea at Chartwell he wore his Arabian robes.

117

In 1908 Winston was best man at his brother's wedding. Just before it he was nearly killed during a house fire. 'Whole rooms sprang into flame as by enchantment,' he wrote. Winston saved his possessions by throwing them out the window – and then put on a fire helmet and went to work battling the flames.

118 Winston personally witnessed Black Tuesday, the Wall Street Crash, during an American tour: 'Under my window,' he wrote, 'a gentleman cast himself down fifteen storeys and was dashed to pieces.' Churchill himself lost £40,000 in the crash (eight years' pay for the Prime Minister at the time).

119 He was hit by a car in New York in 1931: only his thick fur overcoat saved him from serious injury. 'I do not understand why I was not broken like an egg-shell or squashed like a gooseberry,' he wrote. The man who hit him, Mario Constasino, left the hospital with a signed copy of one of Churchill's books.

120 *Finest Hour 059* gives this list of Churchill's accidents and ailments: 'He fell out of a tree (1893), nearly drowned in Lake Lausanne (1893), fell off a camel (1921), fell off a polo pony (1922), fell into a lake while goose hunting (1928) ... He had car accidents in Whitehall, Cairo and Kent ... He had five attacks of pneumonia, suffered from gastroenteritis, appendicitis (1922), tonsillitis (1928), paratyphoid (1932) and irritations of the skin, eyes and lungs. However, he never suffered from nicotine or alcohol poisoning...'

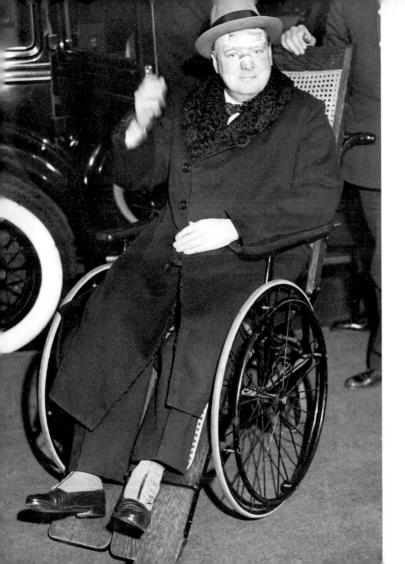

121

Churchill's granddaughter Celia Sandys (*From Winston with Love and Kisses*) reveals that Winston may have suffered from a balance problem, explaining his frequent accidents.

Love,
Family and
Clementine

CHAPTER
THREE

122

Churchill proposed to three different women – Pamela Plowden, Ethel Barrymore and Muriel Wilson – before he proposed to Clementine.

123

Winston was not Clementine's first choice of partner either: she was engaged three times before she married Winston, twice to the grandson of Sir Robert Peel (the man who first established the Metropolitan Police Force at Scotland Yard).

124

According to her mother's letters, Clementine may have been the illegitimate daughter of a champion jockey, 'Bay' Middleton. Others claim that Clementine's father was Algernon Bertram Freeman-Mitford, her aunt's husband and grandfather of the Mitford sisters.

125

Winston proposed to Clementine during a rainstorm, in the ornamental Greek temple at Blenheim Palace.

126

Winston and Clementine married at St Margaret's, Westminster, on 12 September 1908. The church, next to Westminster Abbey, is where Sir Walter Raleigh is buried.

127

Winston's old headmaster, by then the Very Revd the Dean of Manchester Cathedral James Welldon, gave the address at the Churchills' wedding.

128

Winston and Clementine had five children: Diana ('puppy-kitten' or 'P.K.'), Randolph ('Chumbolly'), Sarah ('Bumble Bee'), Marigold ('Duckadilly') and Mary. Sadly, Marigold died when she was only two years and nine months old.

129

Winston & Clementine shares one adorable family game: Bear. Winston would climb a tree. His children would bash each trunk as they passed, crying out 'Bear! Bear!' When they reached the right tree Winston would suddenly, 'with bear-like noises', leap down and chase them.

130

Clementine's nickname for Winston was 'pug' or 'pig'; his for her was 'cat', 'Kat' or 'pussy-cat'. The children were collectively known as the kittens.

131

Talking of cats, No. 10 Annexe's ferocious Persian Smokey once bit Churchill on the toe whilst he was on the phone with Sir Alan Brooke, causing him to roar 'get OFF, you fool!' down the line.

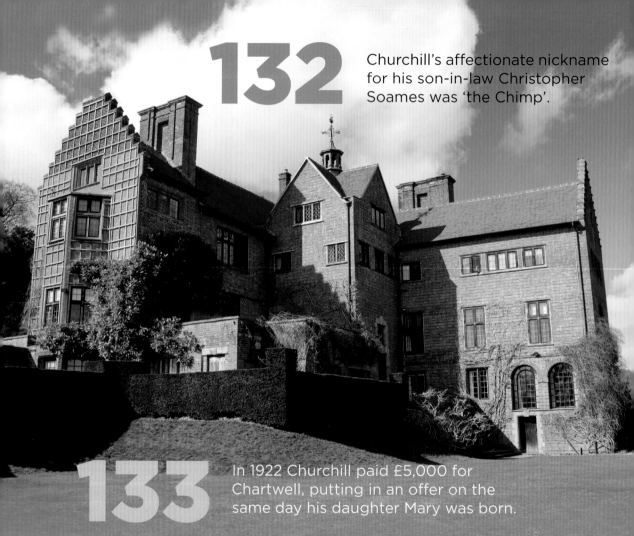

132 Churchill's affectionate nickname for his son-in-law Christopher Soames was 'the Chimp'.

133 In 1922 Churchill paid £5,000 for Chartwell, putting in an offer on the same day his daughter Mary was born.

134

In March 1926 Clementine had tea with Mussolini. He 'has the most charming smile,' she wrote, 'and the most beautiful golden brown piercing eyes ... I am sure he is a very great person – I do hope nothing happens to him.' Il Duce sent her a signed photograph as a keepsake.

135

Churchill's Bodyguard has a great story about Winston's visit to Mussolini: told he couldn't smoke, Churchill put out his cigar, stepped into the huge marble hall of Il Duce's office – and immediately lit another; 'When the cigar had a po⸱⸱⸱rful head of smoke, he began the long walk.'

136

Clementine was an exceptional tennis player. She once took four games from the seven-times Wimbledon ladies' singles champion Dorothea Katherine Douglass, and won the Cannes Lawn Tennis Mixed Doubles Handicap in 1922 and 1923.

137

In 1934 Clementine went on a 30,000 mile South Sea voyage with Walter Guinness, 1st Baron Moyne. The trip brought the first living Komodo dragon to Britain for London Zoo.

138

Clementine and Winston were married for more than fifty-six years. His valet Norman later wrote, 'I have known him select a rosebud on a bush in the gardens at Chartwell, watch it day after day, protect it from rain and insects – just so that it became a perfect bloom to present to his wife.'

139

Winston and Clementine's letters are ceaselessly romantic. 'My Darling One,' he wrote on 8 April 1963, after fifty-four years of marriage: 'This is only to give you my fondest love and kisses a hundred times repeated. I am a pretty dull and paltry scribbler, but my stick as I write carries my heart along with it. Yours ever and always, W'.

140

Churchill hated the portrait given to him by the Houses of Parliament for his 80th birthday; Clementine secretly destroyed it after his death, not saying a word about it for a decade.

141

Clementine died on 12 December 1977. Sadly, three of her five children pre-deceased her: Marigold, Diana and Randolph. Marigold was buried at Kensal Green; the other two children were buried with their father at Bladon, where they were later joined by Clementine, Sarah, Mary, and her husband, Christopher Soames. A service of thanks was held for Clementine's life in Westminster Abbey on 24 January 1978.

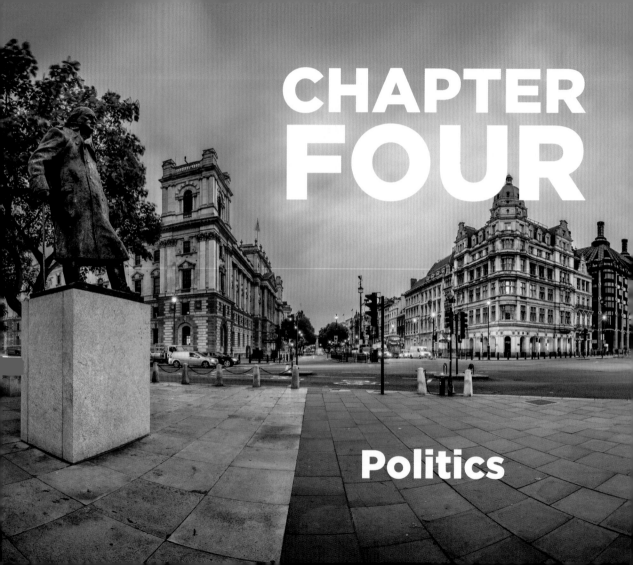

CHAPTER FOUR

Politics

142

Churchill famously quipped that a politician 'is asked to stand, he wants to sit and he is expected to lie.'

143

An outraged politician once asked Churchill, '*Must* you fall asleep when I am speaking?' 'No,' he replied, 'it is purely voluntary.'

144

On running for election, Churchill wrote, 'Of course there are the rowdy meetings. These are a great relief. You have not got to make the same old speech.'

145

The Duke of Devonshire gave Churchill this advice on defeating nerves: 'I have always found it a good rule when you come before a very large audience to take a good look at them and say to yourself with conviction, "I have never seen such a lot of d——d fools in all my life."'

146

Churchill gave his first speech in the House of Commons from the same seat his father had given his last.

147

In 1902 *Punch* magazine listed young Winston's interests as 'the House of Commons – and its reform. The British Army – and its reform. The British Navy – and its reform. The Universe – and its reform.'

CRITICIZING OLD FRIENDS: MR. WINSTON CHURCHILL HECKLING THE GOVERNMENT

148 Winston annoyed his own party so much on 29 March 1904 that the Prime Minister and the entire Cabinet walked out of the House of Commons in the middle of his speech.

149 On 22 April 1904, mid-speech in the House of Commons, Churchill reached the words 'and it rests with those who' – and then stopped. A dreadful silence fell, in which Winston, totally lost for words, sank to his seat and cradled his head in his hands. He never spoke without notes again.

150 Crossing the floor from the Tory to the Liberal benches earned him the nickname 'the Blenheim rat'.

151 When he crossed back again, he commented, 'Anyone can rat, but it takes a certain ingenuity to re-rat.'

152

According to
Tom Hickman's book
Churchill's Bodyguard,
Walter Thompson got
into so many fights
defending Churchill
during his rowdy
Westminster campaign
that he lost 20lbs,
ending the contest with
a pair of black eyes.

153

Churchill slept with a pistol under his pillow in 1921 after receiving death threats; he received more than 700 on one trip alone.

154

Churchill laid the foundations for National Insurance, old-age pensions, job centres and the minimum wage.

155

Churchill introduced the great British tea break in his Shops Bill of 1911.

156

During Churchill's time as Home Secretary his office hanged twenty-two men, including Dr Hawley Harvey Crippen. Churchill's mother attended Crippen's trial.

157 'Please be kind,' Clementine once wrote, 'to the poor boy of 18 who jumped over the gaol wall at Bedford & swam twice across the Ouse followed by every policeman in the town & was finally caught when he fell down from exhaustion.'

158 The designation 'political prisoner' is Churchill's innovation.

159 Churchill was extremely unpopular with Suffragettes, one of whom even whipped him at Bristol Temple Meads station, crying, 'Take *that* in the name of the insulted women of England!' She then attempted to push him under a train. Clementine had to leap over a pile of luggage to grab his coat-tails.

160 A male suffragist called Hugh Franklin once struck him on the Bradford-London train, calling, 'take that, you dirty cur!'

161

Suffragettes also smashed all his windows, and struck him on the head as he entered the House of Commons. They disrupted his speeches with peals of church bells, and he was personally heckled, twice, by Christabel Pankhurst.

162

'Painful scenes were witnessed in the Free Trade Hall,' Churchill later wrote, 'when Miss Christabel Pankhurst, tragical and dishevelled, was finally ejected after having thrown the meeting into pandemonium.'

163

Lady Constance Bulwer-Lytton, the aristocratic suffragette who went to prison under the alias Jane Wharton, was the sister-in-law of Winston's first love Pamela Plowden. She famously cut the letter V (for votes) over her own heart with a hairpin.

164

Churchill's children Diana and Randolph had police protection to stop them from being kidnapped by Suffragettes.

165

In February 1913 Winston warned Clementine not to open 'suspicious parcels' in case they contained a Suffragette bomb. 'These Harpies are quite capable of trying to burn us out,' he wrote.

166

Newly enfranchised female voters were said to be behind Winston's election defeat in 1922: 'The women put Winston out,' Lord Esher commented. 'When he loses his temper he looks so damn ugly!'

167

However, Churchill later declared, 'When I think of what women did in the war I feel sure they deserve to be treated equally.'

168

Churchill wore a fur-lined coat and a top hat to the Siege of Sidney Street in 1911, where he helped to besiege an armed gang of burglars who'd murdered three London policemen.

169

In 1922 Churchill fought his election from an 'invalid chair' after an attack of appendicitis. He was beaten by a Prohibitionist called Scrymgeour. 'In a twinkling of an eye I found myself without an office, without a seat, without a party, and without an appendix,' he wrote.

170

Churchill wore his father's robes as Chancellor of the Exchequer: his mother had refused to hand them back, declaring, 'I am keeping these for my son.'

171

Churchill caused a scandal in December 1936 by speaking up for his dear friend Edward VIII before his abdication.

172

Churchill was a pensioner by the time he finally became Prime Minister: he was sixty-five. The second time he took the office he was even older: seventy-seven.

173

In 1953 he suffered a serious stroke. He still held a meeting of his Cabinet the next day.

THE ILLUSTRATED LONDON NEWS

The World Copyright of all the Editorial Matter, both Illustrations and Letterpress, is Strictly Reserved in Great Britain, the British Dominions and Colonies, Europe, and the United States of America.

SATURDAY, NOVEMBER 3, 1951.

MR. WINSTON CHURCHILL'S FIRST TERM OF OFFICE AS PRIME MINISTER IN PEACETIME: THE LEADER OF THE CONSERVATIVE PARTY, WITH MRS. CHURCHILL, AFTER HEARING THE DECLARATION OF THE POLL AT WOODFORD.

In his last major speech of the election campaign, at Plymouth on October 23, Mr. Churchill replied to the "cruel and ungrateful accusation" that he was a warmonger, and in a restrained and dignified speech said that he remained in public life because, rightly or wrongly, but sincerely, he believed that he might be able to make an important contribution to the prevention of a third world war, and to bringing nearer that lasting peace settlement which the masses of people of every race and in every land fervently desired. "I pray, indeed," he said, "that I may have this opportunity. It is the last prize I ask to win." Mr. Churchill was returned as Member of Parliament for Woodford with a majority of 18,579, the seventh time he has represented the constituency. Later, addressing a crowd outside the house of Sir James Hawkey, chairman of the Woodford Conservative Association, he paid tribute to the part Mrs. Churchill had played in "what we must regard in Woodford as a glorious victory." On October 26 Mr. Attlee tendered his resignation as Prime Minister to the King, who then sent for Mr. Churchill and asked him to form a new administration. Mr. Churchill accepted.

CHAPTER
FIVE

First
World War

174

Churchill personally visited the German Army with the Kaiser before the outbreak of the First World War: once in 1906, and again in 1909. The Kaiser, he wrote, 'talked to foreign visitors with the freedom and manner of an agreeable host at an English country-house party.'

175

Churchill was one of the first Brits to learn to fly, taking to the air 'nearly 140 times' before the First World War and crashing on more than one occasion.

176

Churchill helped to create and develop what became the Royal Naval Air Service from 1911 to 1915. The word 'seaplane' is his invention. However, the word 'aeroplane' was disliked by Churchill: he insisted on the word 'aircraft' in all of his memos.

177

'The air is an extremely dangerous, jealous and exacting mistress,' he later wrote. 'Once under her spell, most lovers are faithful to the end, which is not always old age.'

178

Churchill's flying instructor was killed the day after Churchill's first lesson.

179

Another seaplane crashed the very afternoon he had flown in it, killing all three passengers. His dual-control training machine later 'smashed itself to pieces on the ground'; only 'the press of public business' had prevented Churchill from being in it when it did.

180

After the war Churchill flew with air ace Jack Scott. On one occasion they began to plummet towards the ground, smoke curling from the fuselage. 'What's the matter?' Churchill asked. 'We've been on fire,' his companion calmly replied. 'I've put it out.' He'd let go of the controls, leant out the window and doused the flames with a fire extinguisher.

181

Another time his plane flipped right over on the landing strip, leaving Churchill 'hanging head downwards': 'we were very lucky to escape serious injury,' he wrote, 'either from the shock or from an explosion of fire following upon it.'

182

He once crashed straight into the ground: black and blue, he gave a talk at an official dinner two hours later.

183 Churchill once flew over the trenches of France: 'at 7,000 feet nothing but the fat bulges of big shells bursting far below and the barrages of shrapnel indicated anything unusual in the landscape.'

184 Pioneering British aviator Gustav Hamel was lost in the Channel whilst travelling to give a demonstration for Churchill and his pilots at Portsmouth.

185 From July 1917, as Minister for Munitions, he was 'in charge of the design, manufacture and supply of all kinds of aircraft and air material needed for the War.' He was also Air Minister from 1919 to 1921.

186 Clementine was also an early flier, taking to the air in a biplane in 1913.

187 During the Second World War Churchill even took the controls of his own B24X-bomber transport, 'much,' according to his RAF navigator, 'to the consternation of the passengers who were thrown around in the back.'

188

Winston Churchill helped to invent the tank, which he originally dubbed 'the land ship', after a H.G. Wells short story, *The Land Ironclads*. Tank comes from 'water tanks', the description the factory workers used to stop the Germans discovering what they were really making.

189

Churchill personally oversaw the expansion of the Royal Navy before the war, introducing 15in guns and oil-powered engines to his ships. He installed an enormous world map on his office wall when First Lord of the Admiralty, marked daily with the position of every German ship.

BACK THEM UP!

190

The whole Fleet was ready the moment the war began because Churchill had just deployed the Naval Reserves on a test mobilisation; he held them in position until war was declared.

191

When the sound of Big Ben chiming 11 p.m. reached his office, Churchill personally signalled the Fleet: 'Commence hostilities against Germany'.

192 Churchill commanded the force that held Antwerp from 3 October until 6 October, delaying the German Army and most probably saving Ypres, Dunkirk and Calais from falling into German hands.

193 Clementine gave birth whilst Winston was defending Antwerp.

194 During the war Churchill wrote a letter for his wife to read in the event of his death: 'Do not grieve for me too much ... Death is only an incident, and not the most important.'

195 Churchill's brother Jack fought at Gallipoli. His troops, amused by his tiny shorts, named him 'Lady Constance'.

196

Churchill was agonised by the failure of the Gallipoli campaign for the rest of his life: 'I thought he would die of grief,' Clementine later said.

197

After the disaster in the Dardanelles, Churchill lost his parliamentary position and went to fight in the trenches, going into No Man's Land thirty-six times.

198

Lt Hakewill Smith later described the 'nerve-wracking experience' of going out with Churchill: 'He was like a baby elephant out in No Man's Land at night.'

199

Martin Gilbert's *Churchill: A Life* contains a fantastic story about Churchill in No Man's Land: he and his men had leapt into a shell-hole to avoid a German machine-gunner when a sudden blaze ('put that bloody light out!') gave away their position. Churchill had accidentally sat on his own torch and switched it on.

200

Churchill spent his forty-first birthday under fire in a trench in France.

201

In 1916, Churchill and Hitler occupied trenches just 10 miles apart.

202

Churchill's hatter Lock & Co. personally fitted his steel helmet.

MARCH 22, 1916   THE SKETCH.   249

THE COLONEL AND HIS NEW "NUT" (EVERY APOLOGY!)

COLONEL WINSTON CHURCHILL IN A SHRAPNEL-PROOF HELMET — AND OTHER STUDIES OF HIS HEADGEAR.

203

The kit Churchill had with him when he first reached a trench comprised of his uniform, a hat, a Colt .45 (engraved with his name), one pair of spare socks and a razor.

204

Churchill and his fellow soldiers dried their hosiery in 'the sockatorium'.

205

Churchill wrote from France to describe the 'filth and rubbish everywhere', the 'graves built into the defences ... feet & clothing breaking through the soil', and the sight of 'troops of enormous rats'. 'No one was ever dry or warm,' he wrote.

206

Churchill later commanded the 6th Royal Scots Fusiliers at Ploegsteert in Belgium, known to the Brits as 'Plugstreet'. He remained in command for 100 days, losing 138 men over that time.

207

His first command speech in the trenches went like this: 'Gentlemen, I am now your commanding officer. Those who support me I will look after. Those who go against me I will break. Good afternoon, gentlemen!'

208

Churchill took a tin bathtub and a boiler to his command at the Front. Once his bath was ruined by a shell bursting near his HQ's roof, sending soot pouring down the chimney and over him.

209 Churchill put all of his men at the Front into huge baths made from empty beer vats; 'War is declared, gentlemen,' he said, 'on the lice!'

210 Once a shell blew up his dug-out just five minutes after he'd left it, killing the man inside.

211 On another occasion a bomb fell through his headquarters' roof: a large piece of shrapnel landed less than 2in from his wrist.

212 A colleague later wrote, 'there was no such thing as fear in him'. Another wrote, 'he never fell when a shell went off; he never ducked when a bullet went past.'

213 'I am firmly convinced that no more popular officer [than Churchill] ever commanded troops,' another soldier wrote.

214

Churchill was in his Ministry of Munitions office when the war ended, hearing Big Ben chime the Armistice at 11 a.m.

215

Twenty fortunate people stood on Churchill's car and cheered as it drove slowly through Whitehall on Armistice Day.

216

Churchill was so successful as Minister for Munitions that the US awarded him the Army Distinguished Service Medal, a rare honour, for his success in supplying the US Army with weaponry.

CHAPTER
SIX

Second
World War

217

Churchill called the Munich Pact with the Nazis 'sordid, squalid, sub-human and suicidal'.

218

Churchill was fired from the *Evening Standard* in the run-up to the Second World War for being 'too hard on the Nazis', as Boris Johnson's biography reveals.

219

When Winston became First Lord of the Admiralty again in September 1939, a signal was sent to every ship in the Fleet: 'Winston is back!'

220

The Admiralty office furnishings from Churchill's first term as First Lord of the Admiralty (including a favourite lamp and desk) were reinstalled in his office for his second term. He even found his original wall map behind the sofa.

221

Churchill became Prime Minister on 10 May 1940. He wrote, 'I felt as if I were walking with destiny, and that all my past life had been but a preparation for this hour and this trial.'

222

Churchill's 'last consoling thought' to the 'unenslavable men' of the Home Guard in the case of a German invasion was this: 'you can always take one with you'.

223

On 25 July 1935 Churchill attended the Committee for the Scientific Survey of Air Defence meeting which announced the successful invention of RADAR.

224

The V sign, standing for either the French *victoire* (victory) or Dutch *vrijheid* (freedom), started as a BBC announcement. It sparked a wave of V-shaped graffiti across occupied Europe.

225

The Nazis tried to reclaim the V sign as *viktoria*, ancient German for victory, and hoisted a huge letter 'V' up the Eiffel Tower. Churchill declared that it instead stood for *verloren*, German for defeat.

226

Defiantly, the V on the clock in Churchill's Cabinet War Rooms was (and is) highlighted in red.

227

Churchill's first broadcast as PM began with the famous line, 'I have nothing to offer but blood, toil, sweat and tears'.

228

There is a story that Churchill ended his 4 June 1940 speech in the House ('we shall fight them on the beaches') by muttering, 'We'll fight them with the butt end of broken beer bottles because that's all we've bloody well got.'

THE PRIME MINISTER INSPECTING THE RUINED HOUSE OF COMMONS.

AMIDST A HIDEOUS CONFUSION OF TWISTED GIRDERS, BLOCKS OF STONE AND CHARRED WOODWORK, MR. CHURCHILL SURVEYS THE MOTHER OF PARLIAMENTS, BOMBED DELIBERATELY ON MAY 10 BY GERMAN RAIDERS. ON THE RIGHT IS LORD REITH.

The Prime Minister, accompanied by Lord Reith, Lord Beaverbrook, and Mrs. Churchill, inspecting the damage done on Saturday night, May 10, to the Chamber of Commons, is seen standing pensively on what was the floor of the House, looking towards the Ministerial benches from which he delivered so many great orations. In the background is the entrance from behind the Speaker's Chair. Not an atom of woodwork remains of the structure. The blanched walls lie open to the sky, and there is nothing to show where the various galleries overlooking the Chamber stood.

The building was hit by an oil-bomb, followed by three or four high-explosives, and many incendiaries, which also set alight the historic roof of Westminster Hall. The bomb damage to the Houses of Parliament, the Abbey, and surroundings, was not indiscriminate. "It resulted," says the "Daily Telegraph," "from a deliberate attack, obviously planned and maintained for two hours." An emergency home for the Mother of Parliaments is ready and, in fact, has been already used. The King opened the new Session there last November. [C.P.U.]

229

Churchill visited the Houses of Parliament in 1941 after they were (as he put it) 'blown to smithereens' by a Nazi bomb. One reporter noted the tears that ran down his face as he surveyed the damage.

230

He also frequently wept when he saw the impact of the Blitz. 'You see, he really cares; he's crying,' said one elderly witness.

231 Churchill had lunch with the King, to discuss the progress of the war, every Tuesday. Once Churchill and the King had dinner in the air-raid shelter underneath No. 10's back garden. Churchill popped outside several times during the heavy raid, 'to see how things are going.'

232 In October 1941 the Treasury building was hit by a bomb whilst Churchill was eating dinner at No. 10. If Churchill hadn't ordered his kitchen staff into an air-raid shelter when the raid began they would have been killed.

233 Chartwell had an air-raid shelter with room for ten people. In February 1945 a rocket burst over the house. Clementine wrote: '[we] picked up masses of sharp aluminum fragments all over the garden, tennis court and garage yard.'

234 Churchill liked to take 'constitutionals' in St James's Park during the blackout: his bodyguard made him a special torch-holder for the top of his walking stick.

235 He also loved to walk during an air raid; once he was just missed by a 1,000lb bomb, which hit the pavement behind him and wrecked the water main, drenching him.

236 Churchill's bodyguard later described Churchill's 'total disregard for danger as he walked the streets when bombs were falling': 'I have asked the people of this country to carry on,' Churchill said. 'If you think I am going to hide in an air-raid shelter, not for you or anyone else will I do it.'

237 He visited anti-aircraft sites during heavy raids, refusing an armoured car: 'I will not have any privileges. I will take the same chance as anyone else.'

238 Churchill's car was once lifted by an explosion: it ran along on two wheels before it righted itself.

239 Churchill tried three times to see a V-1 rocket ('flies', to the PM) in action, but each time his bodyguard foiled him.

240

Shrapnel once whistled through the Annexe's door, wounding one of Churchill's detectives. If his bodyguard Walter Thompson hadn't pushed him behind the door Churchill would have been struck in the stomach.

241

Somewhat ironically, Churchill's bodyguard carried a German Luger handgun towards the end of the war.

242

Churchill visited Hitler's bunker after his suicide and was photographed sitting in Hitler's chair. The petrol cans used to burn the Führer's body were still clearly visible.

243

Churchill's deliberately pronounced Nazi 'Naaarzi' as a sign of defiance. He referred to Hitler as 'Herr Schicklgruber', Hitler's family name.

244

Churchill's response to news of the failed Stauffenberg bombing on 20 July 1944 was short and to the point: 'They missed the old bugger,' he said.

245 Churchill signed his letters to President Roosevelt 'Former Naval Person'.

246 Richard Holmes estimated that Churchill and Roosevelt wrote 1,700 letters and telegrams to each other, roughly one for every day he was Prime Minister.

247 In 1940 Roosevelt commented, 'As long as that old bastard's in charge, Britain will never surrender.'

248 Churchill suffered a minor heart attack during his Christmas visit to the White House in December 1941.

249 In December 1943, at Tunis, Churchill was struck down with pneumonia. 'Don't worry,' he told his daughter Sarah, 'it doesn't matter if I die now – the plans for victory have been laid, and it's only a matter of time.'

250 Sarah Churchill entertained her father during his illness in 1943 by reading *Pride and Prejudice* to him; he remarked that Clementine was 'so like' Elizabeth.

251 In January 1943 Churchill said farewell to Roosevelt at Marrakesh whilst wearing his favourite dressing gown: green and gold with red dragons on it.

252 Churchill once appeared quite naked at the White House, telling the astonished Roosevelt, as he entered Churchill's bedroom, 'As you see, the British Prime Minister has nothing to hide from the President of the United States.'

253

Churchill also bathed naked at Palm Beach. When his bodyguard told him he could be seen through binoculars, he replied, 'If they are that much interested, it is their own fault what they see.'

254 Talking of nudity, he once shook hands with a young Prince Charles whilst wearing nothing but a shirt and pants.

255 He frequently strolled past the maid on the way to his bath. He would take his cigar out of his mouth, wish her good morning, and carry on, quite naked, into the bathroom.

256 Churchill would sometimes offer a 'stately greeting' (as his secretary Elizabeth Nel put it) to a visitor as he paraded from bathroom to bedroom at the No. 10 Annexe, 'wrapped only in a huge bath towel [and] looking like one of the later Roman Emperors,' according to Martin Gilbert.

257 Churchill instigated the George Medal and the George Cross for acts of bravery.

258

Churchill flew over Dunkirk as the evacuation was ongoing; according to Tom Hickman's *Churchill's Bodyguard*, he went without an air escort to save planes to protect the ships.

259

Churchill tried his utmost to sail as part of the first wave of the D-Day force: in the end the King himself had to ban him from going, relenting only on the sixth day of the attack.

DESERVE VICTORY !

260 Churchill later watched 14,000 parachutists land in France from aboard a destroyer.

261 The Commandos were Churchill's suggestion (men to launch his famous 'butcher and bolt' policy), as were the Parachute Regiment.

262 Churchill's son Randolph later fought with the SAS.

263 The Second World War Union Jack flag hanging in Churchill's office at Chartwell was the first to fly over a liberated town in Europe.

"NEVER WAS SO MUCH OWED BY SO MANY TO SO FEW"

THE PRIME MINISTER

264

Churchill came up with the line 'never in the field of human conflict has so much been owed by so many to so few' in the car on the way to Chequers, having spent the afternoon watching the Battle of Britain from an RAF bunker at Uxbridge.

265

Churchill's speeches were typed into 'speech form', to help with emphasis:

Never in the field of human conflict
Was so much owed
By so many
To so few

266

Churchill's phone in No. 10 was a green colour, to indicate that the line was scrambled to help disrupt attempts at espionage. It had direct lines to Buckingham Palace and the House of Commons.

267

No. 10's top-secret phone number during the war was 'Rapid Falls 4466'.

268 Every single phone call to or by Churchill (as with all callers at his level) began with an announcement: 'The enemy is recording your conversation ... Great discretion is necessary. Any indiscretion will be reported by the Censor to the highest authority.' Churchill told his Censor to hurry up.

269 Churchill ended all his phone calls with KBO: Keep Buggering On.

270 Churchill's codename for phone calls was either 'John Martin' (his private secretary) or 'Mr White'; Roosevelt was 'Mr Smith'. Clementine was known as 'the Colonel'.

271 Churchill's phone room in the Cabinet War Rooms was a former broom cupboard disguised as a toilet: the sign on the door read either 'engaged' or 'vacant'.

272 There were in fact no flushing toilets in the Cabinet War Rooms.

273 The phone is a replica: Churchill bashed his on the table whenever the connection was bad, and eventually it broke.

274 The Germans cracked the A3 Scrambler that protected British-American phone calls, and listened to Churchill's coded conversations with Roosevelt.

275 A new system – 'Sigsaly', vetted by Dr Alan Turing of Enigma fame – prevented the conversations from being tapped but was not often used: it made Churchill's voice sound 'like Donald Duck', as his Censor Ruth Ive put it.

276 The main unit of Sigsaly was housed in the basement of Selfridges.

277

Churchill's personal codename for ENIGMA messages was Boniface; Bletchley was the 'geese that laid golden eggs and never cackled'.

278

Sir Alan Brooke, Chief of Imperial Staff, later joked that the Cabinet War Rooms 'was in every way an excellent battle headquarters, with only one fault, namely its proximity to Winston!'

279 Churchill couldn't abide unnecessary noise, especially the sound of whistling – not even of his favourite tune, 'Run, Rabbit, Run'. Signs were posted in Churchill's War Rooms: 'There is to be no whistling or unnecessary noise in this passage.'

280 In order to reduce the distracting clatter, Churchill's staff worked on specially imported noiseless typewriters.

281 The War Rooms were not bomb-proof: a bomb striking St James's Park at an angle would have crashed straight into the complex. Luckily, only the steps outside the modern entrance were ever hit.

282 If a bomb had hit the War Rooms there was the very real possibility that everyone inside would have drowned, as the complex was below the level of the Thames.

283

Churchill watched air raids from the roof of the War Rooms.

284

The walls of the War Rooms were hung with rifles in case Nazis parachuted in to attack. Sixty Royal Marines were on guard inside.

285 The switchboard operators in the Cabinet War Rooms were issued with specially adapted gas masks so they could keep working through a gas attack.

286 Staff spent so long – up to eighteen hours a day – in the gloom of the War Rooms that they had to be treated with sun lamps to ward off rickets and other disorders.

287 Churchill's pseudonym for incognito visits to the various war zones was 'Colonel Kent' or 'Colonel Warden'. He had his own specially equipped train for touring the UK during the war.

288 Winston announced the end of the war, from the same room Chamberlain had announced its outbreak, with the words, 'Advance Britannia! Long live the cause of freedom! God save the King!'

289 Clementine was in Russia when the war ended. She sent her husband a telegram which read: 'All my thoughts are with you on this supreme day my darling. It could not have happened without you. All my love, Clemmie.'

290 Cabinet War Room staff watched the VE-day celebrations from the roof of No. 10 Annexe, above the War Rooms.

291 Churchill himself gave instructions that Britain's pubs were to be fully stocked with beer on VE-Day.

292 Churchill walked down Whitehall on VE-Day. Eventually the crowd of well-wishers proved too dense to travel through. He perched on top of a car roof, whereupon the crowd 'cheered their heads off,' according to witnesses. Churchill's bodyguard was forced to knock people off the running boards to keep them back.

293 The spotlights at the Ministry of Health went out just as Churchill was saying 'the lights went out' in one VE-Day speech, causing the crowd to roar with laughter.

294

Churchill appeared on the balcony of Buckingham Palace with the King and Queen at the end of the war. When he told the crowd it was their victory they roared back, 'No, it's yours!'

295

Harold Nicolson described Churchill's entry into the House of Commons at the war's end: 'Then a slight stir was observed behind the Speaker's chair, and Winston, looking coy and cheerful, came in. The House rose as a man, and yelled and yelled and waved their Order Papers. He responded, not with a bow exactly, but with an odd shy jerk of the head and with a wide grin.'

CHAPTER
SEVEN

Churchill,
the Man

296

Winston Churchill was a redhead.

297

He was short: sources give his height as between 5ft 6in and 5ft 8in.

298

He did not go to university, but was awarded twenty honorary degrees in later life. Winston was also awarded honorary American citizenship by John F. Kennedy in 1963 (only the second person in history): 'his 'bravery, charity and valor, both in war and in peace, have been a flame of inspiration in freedom's darkest hour', said the award, and 'his life has shown that no adversary can overcome, and no fear can deter, free men in the defense of their freedom.'

299

Churchill habitually took breakfast in bed, reading the papers (including the Communist *Daily Worker*) and marking up sections of interest to show his wife.

300

Norman McGowan, Churchill's valet in the later years of Winston's life, initially raced Mrs Churchill's maid every morning for the paper; the first Churchill got to read in bed, whilst the other had to wait for single pages as and when they were finished.

301

For eight days in 1926, whilst all British printers were on strike, Churchill actually ran his own newspaper: the *British Gazette*. The press was smashed by an agitator with a crowbar; Churchill sent the broken section to the Royal Navy, who returned it 'all shined up, wrapped in bunting and with a Union Jack sticking out of her top' (according to Churchill's bodyguard).

302 A light Churchill breakfast, according to the Churchill Museum, 'might consist of melon, omelette, or bacon and eggs, followed by a cutlet or leg of chicken, toast, marmalade and coffee.'

303 After breakfast Churchill would work in bed. Intriguingly, Churchill hated paperclips: he punched holes in his papers with his 'klop' instead.

304 Clementine used to sneak into Winston's bedroom and put his clock forward, in an attempt to make him appear at meals on time.

305 The valet had a clever trick to get him out of bed for lunch: he would ring the doorbell, and then run into Churchill's room to announce that guests had arrived.

306 After lunch Churchill would take a one-hour power nap, even at the Houses of Parliament; a large bed came on election tours with him. He always slept in a black silk eye-mask.

307 After lunch, more work until dinner at 6 p.m. At midnight he'd gather his secretaries and start again; during the Second World War he could work as late as 4.30 a.m. His secretaries would be up until as late as 6 a.m. typing up their copies.

308 One year his secretary expressed her surprise that he expected her by 8 a.m. on Christmas Day. 'Oh well,' Churchill amended, 'make it 8.30.'

309 Another Churchill Christmas was spent on a light cruiser off the coast of Greece. Hilariously, the British sailors, who wore festive fancy dress, gave the poor confused Greek Archbishop an enormous cheer when he came aboard in his cope and hat.

310

The last thing Churchill did at night was brush his remaining strands straight over his ears: 'That's the only way to keep your hair,' he told his valet.

311

Winston once replied, when asked how he'd like his hair cut, 'A man of my limited resources can't be choosy.'

312

There are many examples of Churchill's kindness. For example, he paid for the funeral of Mr 'Donkey' Jack, a gypsy who lived on common land near Chartwell; he then invited Mrs 'Donkey' Jack to move into Chartwell's woods after she was evicted from her home by the council.

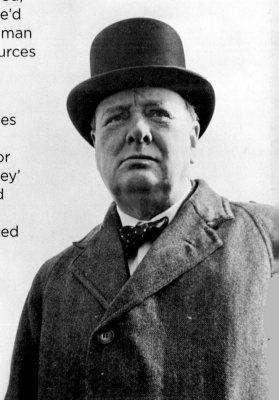

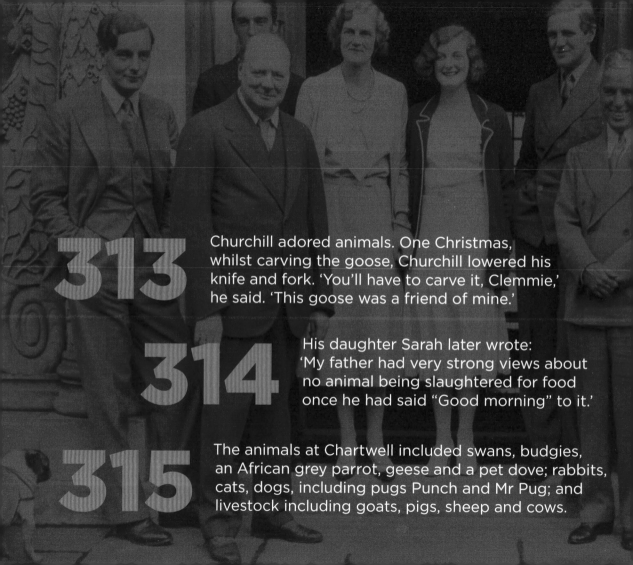

313 Churchill adored animals. One Christmas, whilst carving the goose, Churchill lowered his knife and fork. 'You'll have to carve it, Clemmie,' he said. 'This goose was a friend of mine.'

314 His daughter Sarah later wrote: 'My father had very strong views about no animal being slaughtered for food once he had said "Good morning" to it.'

315 The animals at Chartwell included swans, budgies, an African grey parrot, geese and a pet dove; rabbits, cats, dogs, including pugs Punch and Mr Pug; and livestock including goats, pigs, sheep and cows.

316 Churchill's chickens lived in a shed, built by Winston, called 'Chickenham Palace'.

317 Churchill's beloved pet fish were hand-fed on maggots specially imported from Yorkshire.

318 No official dinner could begin at Chartwell until Rufus, his beloved poodle, had finished eating *his* dinner at Churchill's feet.

319 Occasionally he'd step out of a Commons debate to get an update on how Rufus was doing at home.

320 Churchill used to cover Rufus's eyes during *Oliver Twist*, in the part where Sikes tries to kill his dog Bullseye: 'Don't look now, dear,' he'd say. 'I'll tell you all about it afterwards.'

321

The first Rufus was let off his lead by a maid and was killed by a car; Rufus II then replaced him. Both dogs used to sleep on Churchill's bed from time to time.

322

Churchill started his day with a blend of whisky, ice and soda water just after breakfast; he also drank a pint of champagne every day, plus white wine at lunch and dinner, and port or brandy in the evening.

323

As a thank you for the liberation of France, only Winston Churchill was allowed to buy Pol-Roger 1928. Their 1982 vintage cuvée is named after him, and their black labels are a tribute to Churchill's passing by his friend Odette Pol-Roger.

324 Pol-Roger paid to replace Chartwell's trees after the Great Storm of 1988 knocked them all flat. *Finest Hour* 060 includes an irresistible joke about this: 'For even if those trees last a thousand years, men will still say, "this was their finest bower."'

325 Churchill once turned down an offer of £2,000 to abstain from drinking for a year, as 'life would not be worth living'.

326 The *Telegraph* obituary of Joe Gilmore, head barman at the Savoy, reported his 'sole charge of Churchill's private bottle of Black & White whisky': Churchill would be served his whisky 'with a knowing nod', whilst his companion Charles de Gaulle would get 'the wartime stuff coloured with teabags'.

327 Winston refused to pay for Clementine's gin; she had to pay for her own bottles.

328

One of Churchill's favourite nightcaps was a bowl of turtle soup.

329

Churchill smoked between eight and ten large Cuban cigars per day. Winston smoked even as a schoolboy, but was introduced to his trademark Havana cigars during his time as a journalist in Cuba.

330

Eight to ten cigars was nothing on his father, Lord Randolph, who smoked forty Turkish roll-ups a day.

331

When Field Marshal Montgomery told him, 'I neither drink nor smoke and am a hundred percent fit,' Winston replied: 'I drink and smoke and am two hundred percent fit.'

332

His lifetime consumption of cigars has been estimated at a quarter of a million. He generally smoked only around half of each, the other half going either to Kearns, the gardener at Chartwell, for his pipe, or to the vendor of his copy of the *Evening Standard* (for which the seller refused to take any payment).

333

He invented a device, a 'bellybando' (a piece of brown paper that went around the end of each), to stop his cigars from dissolving as he chewed on them.

334 Churchill's cigars had their own cellar for safekeeping during the Blitz.

335 Elizabeth Layton, one of his secretaries, later recalled how staff learned not to sit between Churchill and his fire, where he would throw any cigar that did not meet his high standards.

336 If Churchill lit his cigar with a candle then his secretaries had to carry the candle out of the room before blowing it out: Churchill hated the smell of burnt wax.

337 Sometimes he would accidentally throw a lit cigar out of bed and into the waste-paper bin, starting a fire which his valet would then have to douse with the soda syphon.

338 He wore expensive (pink) silk underwear, declaring that this luxury was 'essential to his well-being'.

339 The fabric Poole & Co. used to make Churchill's famous 'Tommy gun' suit is called 'the Churchill'. Customers can order a classic two-piece in the same fabric today.

340

The German press ran the Tommy-gun photograph with the slogan 'wanted for incitement to murder', calling Churchill a 'gangster' and claiming his aim was to incite 'an absolutely criminal form of warfare' in which 'women, children and ordinary citizens shall take leading parts'.

341

The pattern of his bow-tie (which he wore as a tribute to his father) is still known as the 'Churchill Spot'.

342

Lady Diana Cooper came up with the best description of his famous Siren suits: 'He looks exactly like the good little pig building his house with bricks.'

343

Siren-suited Churchill was once mistaken for an engineer who'd accidentally wandered into the Map Room.

344

Churchill was actually a paid-up member of the Union of Building Trade Workers, and could lay at a rate of a brick a minute.

345 Churchill's first section of wall in his Chartwell cottage was so wonky that his builder and his bodyguard secretly rebuilt it whilst he was at lunch.

346 His gold-topped cane was a wedding present from King Edward VII.

347 Winston's family called his large gold watch 'the Turnip'.

348 An effigy of Winston Churchill first appeared in Madam Tussaud's in 1908, on the day of his wedding. By 1956 his notes read: 'Additional Information: Round back. Head very forward. High shoulders. Corpulent.' His measurements were: chest 44.5in; waist 47in; hips 47in.

349 Churchill weighed 15 stone by May 1954 (or 15.5 on the 'broken-down old' scales at Chartwell). He wrote: 'I have no grievance against a tomato, but I think one should eat other things as well.'

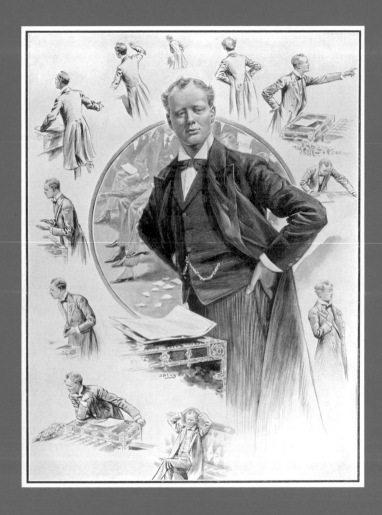

350

Churchill wrote all his own speeches, which, when Chancellor, could be three or four hours long.

351

Churchill practised his early speeches in the mirror, often striking nearby bits of furniture at the key moments.

352

Churchill's memos were called 'Churchill's Prayers' by his secretaries, as he always ended them with 'Pray give me the facts on half a sheet of paper'.

353

He often dictated to his secretaries whilst in the bath, a habit depicted in the glorious 2002 film *The Gathering Storm*. Goebbels recorded that the Führer found this habit 'hugely amusing'.

354 Churchill's valet Norman McGowan once responded to Churchill as he was muttering in his bath. 'I wasn't talking to you, Norman,' Churchill replied. 'I was addressing the House of Commons.'

355 As a schoolboy Churchill dictated a letter to his mother from his bath; a friend was persuaded to write it down for him.

356 As an adult Churchill liked to have two hot baths a day. The Churchills travelled with a canvas bath so Winston could take a dip whenever he fancied.

357 He once took a bath in the middle of a desert; he got the driver to drain the water from his train engine to fill the tub.

358 Once a 'piercing scream' from Churchill's room brought the detectives and his valet running. 'Norman,' he said, 'as I was getting out of the bath I slipped and sat on the hot tap.'

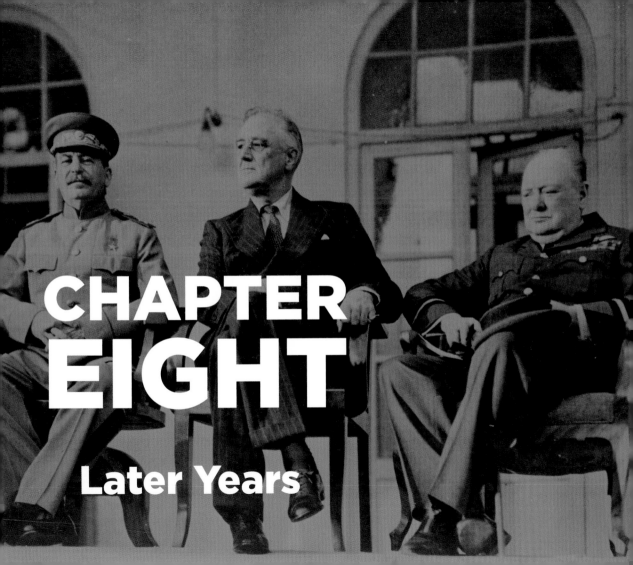

CHAPTER
EIGHT

Later Years

359 Churchill watched the progress of the 1945 election count, which he lost, from the Map Room at the Cabinet War Rooms.

360 Clementine tried to comfort Winston by saying his 1945 loss could be a blessing in disguise. 'At the moment it seems quite effectively disguised,' Churchill replied.

361

Churchill initially turned down the Order of the Garter in 1945, on the grounds that the British public had given him 'the Order of the Boot'.

362

Labour MPs celebrated their victory in the 1945 election by singing 'The Red Flag'. The Conservatives responded with a song for Winston: 'For He's a Jolly Good Fellow'. Churchill's own singing voice was apparently terrible: as one First World War soldier put it, 'he could not sing for nuts'.

363 Churchill took up temporary quarters in the penthouse of Claridges after he lost the 1945 election.

364 Churchill is credited with coining the terms 'Iron Curtain' and 'Middle East'. However, the former phrase was actually used by Germany before Churchill: Goebbels used it in *Das Reich*.

365 When Churchill first used the term 'Iron Curtain' in a conversation with Stalin (who he called 'Uncle Joe'), Stalin replied, 'Fairy tales!'

366 Churchill's first description of Bolshevism was 'a ghoul descending from a pile of skulls.' It was a plague, a pestilence, a fungus, a beast, a crocodile, a bungler, and, best of all, a 'foul baboonery'.

367 Stalin came to Churchill's sixty-ninth birthday party. Amusingly, a waiter tripped during Stalin's toast and dropped a 'magnificent ice-pudding' on his translator's head.

368 Mary Soames, Churchill's daughter, gave an interview to the *Telegraph* (reprinted in *Finest Hour* 116) where she remembered Stalin at the Potsdam conference as 'small, dapper and rather twinkly'.

369 Elizabeth Nel, Churchill's secretary, has the best description of Stalin in his overcoat: 'he reminded me of a rather wicked-looking stuffed doll.'

370 Elizabeth Nel also records that the Russians served caviar and vodka for breakfast during Churchill's Russian visits.

371 Clementine raised more than £7 million for the Red Cross 'Aid to Russia' fund. In gratitude she was escorted on a five-week tour of Russia, where she met Stalin and Molotov (of cocktail fame) and visited the Kremlin.

372 Winston signed important documents using a gold pen from his children. Clementine presented Stalin with a gold pen (a gift from Winston) on her Russian trip; Stalin looked nonplussed. 'I only write with a pencil,' he said.

373

Clementine was presented with the Russian Order of the Red Banner of Labour for her efforts to help the Soviet Union.

374

Churchill was one of the people to sign off on the Manhattan Project. The first nuclear test took place just ten days before he was voted out of office.

375 The British nuclear programme (codenamed Tube Alloys) used screens specially printed for it by Sun Engraving Co., the printer of *Woman's Own* magazine.

376 Churchill imagined the nuclear age in his article 'Shall we all commit suicide?' 'Might not a bomb no bigger than an orange be found to possess a secret power to destroy a whole block of buildings – nay, to concentrate the force of a thousand tons of cordite and blast a township to smoke?'

377 Churchill's first racehorse, Colonist II, won at Ascot and Newmarket. His racing colours were pink and chocolate-brown, as Churchill's father had used.

378 Churchill blamed one fourth place on the fact that his pep talk for Colonist II included the words, 'If you win it … you will spend the rest of your life in agreeable female company'. After that, he said, the horse 'did not keep his mind on the race'.

379 When Colonist II's trainer first suggested putting the horse out to stud (which he did in 1951), Churchill replied: 'To stud? And have it said that the Prime Minister of Great Britain is living on the immoral earnings of a horse?'

380 Churchill raced more than seventy winners in his career.

381 Clementine and Churchill spent their forty-fifth wedding anniversary at the St Leger at Doncaster, as guests of the Queen. They spent the night at Balmoral.

382 On his eighty-fifth birthday one MP muttered to a friend, 'They say he's getting a bit past it.' 'They say the old man's getting deaf as well,' Winston replied.

383 Churchill was an MP until six months before his death. A young photographer once hoped to photograph Churchill on his 100th birthday. 'I don't see why not, young man,' he replied. 'You look reasonably fit and healthy.'

384 He fought his last election campaign on 8 October 1959, at the age of eighty-four.

385 Churchill broke his hip in a fall at Monte Carlo in June of 1962. He told Anthony Montague Browne, 'Remember, I want to die in England. Promise me you will see to it.'

386 In June 1963, despite his fall, Churchill went on the last of his eight cruises with Aristotle Onassis.

387 His last appearance at the House of Commons was on 27 July 1964: more than half a century of service.

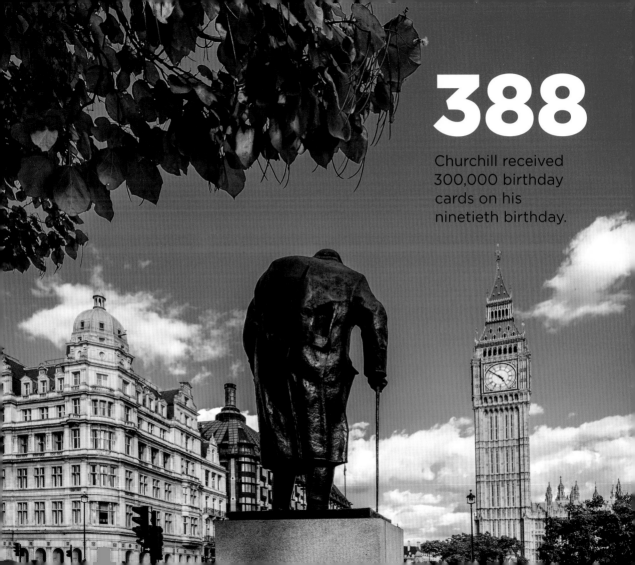

388

Churchill received 300,000 birthday cards on his ninetieth birthday.

389 Churchill helped to plan his own state funeral (which was to be the largest ever held at that time), giving it the codename 'Operation Hope-Not'.

390 Churchill requested that 'The Battle Hymn of the Republic' be sung at his funeral, as it had been at Roosevelt's.

391 Winston died just after 8 a.m. on 24 January 1965. Clementine was holding Winston's hand when he died.

392 His last words were said to have been, 'The journey has been enjoyable and well worth the making – once!'

393

The Queen's message to Clementine on his death read: 'The whole world is poorer by the loss of his many-sided genius, while the survival of this country and the sister nations of the Commonwealth, in the face of the greatest danger that has ever threatened them, will be a perpetual memorial to his leadership, his vision and his indomitable courage.'

394

The flags of every public building (and of Harrow) flew at half-mast to mark his passing. Lloyds of London rang their famous Lutine bell to announce his death, while St Paul's tolled 'Great Tom'.

395

An estimated 4,000 people an hour came to pay their respects to Winston whilst his coffin lay in state at Westminster Hall.

396 All the cranes on the South Bank dipped in tribute as his coffin passed.

397 Winston's coffin was carried to his final resting place behind the locomotive *Winston Churchill*.

398 Only two wreaths were taken to his burial: one read 'To my darling Winston, Clemmie'; the other read, 'From the Nation and Commonwealth, Elizabeth R.'

399 Winston chose the spot for his grave because it was in view of the place he was born.

400 So many people have since visited his grave that they had to replace the gravestone in 1998, and restore it again in 2006.

Short Bibliography

Modern

Young Titan: The Making of Winston Churchill by Michael Shelden

The Churchill Factor: How One Man Made History by Boris Johnson

Winston Churchill: Personal Accounts of the Great Leader at War 1895-1945 by Michael Paterson

My Years With Churchill by Norman McGowan

The Woman Who Censored Churchill by Ruth Ive

Sixty Minutes with Winston Churchill by Ex-Detective-Inspector W.H Thompson

Churchill by Roy Jenkins

Winston Churchill, Soldier: The Life of a Gentleman at War by Douglas S. Russell

His Finest Hour: A Brief Life of Winston Churchill by Christopher Catherwood

Dark Lady: Winston Churchill's Mother and her World by Charles Higham

Churchill Defiant: Fighting on, 1945-1955 by Barbara Leaming

Winston & Clementine: The Triumph of the Churchills by Richard Hough

A Thread in the Tapestry by Sarah Churchill

Churchill: A Life by Martin Gilbert

The Irrepressible Churchill compiled by Kay Halle

Speaking for Themselves: The Personal Letters of Winston and Clementine Churchill edited by their daughter Mary Soames

From Winston With Love and Kisses: The Young Churchill by Celia Sandys

The Reminiscences of Lady Randolph Churchill by Mrs George Cornwallis-West

Churchill's Bodyguard: The Authorized Biography of Walter H. Thompson by Tom Hickman

Mr Churchill's Secretary by Elizabeth Nel

Finest Hour, Journal of the International Churchill Society

Selected Books by Churchill

My Early Life

The River War

Thoughts and Adventures

My African Journey

www.winstonchurchill.org

Picture Credits

Fact 179	Everett Historical, Shutterstock
Fact 181	Library of Congress, LC-USZC4-10231
Fact 188	Vitezslav Halamka, Shutterstock
Fact 189	Mary Evans Picture Library
Fact 190	Everett Historical, Shutterstock
Fact 192	Library of Congress, LC-DIG-ds-07162
Fact 196	Everett Historical, Shutterstock
Fact 198	Library of Congress, LC-DIG-stereo-1s04039
Fact 202	© Illustrated London News Ltd/Mary Evans
Fact 203	Everett Historical, Shutterstock
Fact 206	© Illustrated London News Ltd/Mary Evans
Fact 208	LC-DIG-ggbain-18436, Library of Congress
Fact 214	© Illustrated London News Ltd/Mary Evans
Chapter six	©The National Army Museum/ Mary Evans Picture Library
Fact 217	Library of Congress, LC-USZ62-48839
Fact 219	Library of Congress, LC-USZ62-19266
Fact 221	Mary Evans/Everett Collection
Fact 222	lapas77, Shutterstock
Fact 224	Mary Evans Picture Library
Fact 227	© Illustrated London News Ltd/Mary Evans
Fact 229	© Illustrated London News Ltd/Mary Evans
Fact 242	Mary Evans/The Everett Collection
Fact 243	Library of Congress, LC-DIG-hec-35556
Fact 245	Wellcome Library, London
Fact 253	© Illustrated London News Ltd/Mary Evans
Fact 259	Mary Evans Picture Library
Fact 260	Everett Historical, Shutterstock
Fact 264	Mary Evans Picture Library/ Onslow Auctions Limited
Fact 266	Baimieng, Shutterstock
Fact 277	Everett Historical, Shutterstock
Fact 283	Mary Evans/The Everett Collection
Fact 287	Mary Evans/Everett Collection
Fact 290	© Illustrated London News Ltd/Mary Evans
Fact 294	© Illustrated London News Ltd/Mary Evans
Chapter seven	Mary Evans Picture Library
Fact 296	Mary Evans Picture Library
Fact 301	Everett Historical, Shutterstock
Fact 311	Library of Congress, LC-USW33-019093-C
Fact 315	Everett Collection/Mary Evans
Fact 317	© Illustrated London News Ltd/Mary Evans
Fact 322	Altana8, Shutterstock
Fact 328	Galina Savina, Shutterstock
Fact 329	Malcolm Greensmith © Adrian Bradbury/Mary Evans
Fact 322	© Illustrated London News Ltd/Mary Evans
Fact 339	Mary Evans/SZ Photo/Scherl
Fact 341	Library of Congress, LC-USZ62-65636
Fact 344	© Illustrated London News Ltd/Mary Evans
Fact 350	© Illustrated London News Ltd/Mary Evans
Fact 353	mOleks, Shutterstock
Chapter eight	Library of Congress, LC-USZ62-32833
Fact 360	Mary Evans/Everett Collection
Fact 361	Library of Congress, LC-DIG-ppmsca-05370
Fact 365	steamdesign, Shutterstock
Fact 367	Library of Congress, LC-USZ62-7449
Fact 374	Library of Congress, LC-USZ62-39852
Fact 377	© Illustrated London News Ltd/Mary Evans
Fact 381	Library of Congress, LC-DIG-ppmsc-07532
Fact 388	BigRoloImages, Shutterstock
Fact 393	© Illustrated London News Ltd/Mary Evans
Fact 394	© Illustrated London News Ltd/Mary Evans